TIDELINES

poems by

Russell Steinke

Finishing Line Press
Georgetown, Kentucky

TIDELINES

*For
Roxane
and
Scott Russell
Jocelyn Dawn
Douglas John*

Copyright © 2017 by Russell Steinke
ISBN 978-1-63534-113-3 First Edition
All rights reserved under International and Pan-American Copyright Conventions.
No part of this book may be reproduced in any manner whatsoever without written
permission from the publisher, except in the case of brief quotations embodied in critical
articles and reviews.

ACKNOWLEDGMENTS

These poems appeared, some in different versions, in the literary magazines identified.

The Shallows: *Crucible*
In the Realm of Flowers (as The Flowers): *Confrontation*
Neap Tide: *Epoch*
Clam Digger and section 4 of Neck Road Idyll (as Where?): *Wetlands*
Beachcomber (as Driftwood): *Maelstrom*
Seagulls off Captree Basin: *Island Light*
The Cry: *Shaman*
The Penguins at the Coney Island Aquarium: *Long Pond Review*
Shallows (as There): *The Texas Slough*
Blizzard of '78 at Tucker Flasts (as In Dry Dock): *Icarus*
stones in a stream: *New: American and Canadian Poetry*

Publisher: Leah Maines

Editor: Christen Kincaid

Cover Art: Scott R. Steinke, Tideline PhotoLabs

Author Photo: Scott R. Steinke, Tideline PhotoLabs

Cover Design: Elizabeth Maines McCleavy

Printed in the USA on acid-free paper.
Order online: www.finishinglinepress.com
   also available on amazon.com

Author inquiries and mail orders:
Finishing Line Press
P. O. Box 1626
Georgetown, Kentucky 40324
U. S. A.

Table of Contents

The Swallows 1

In the Realm of Flowers 2

Neap Tide 4

Beachcomber 5

Clam Digger 6

Casting for Sunlight in Flounder Town 8

Still Life with Whelk Shell and Coconut 10

Seagulls off Captree Basin 11

Neck Road Idyll 12

Bay Light 16

Voyages 17

The Cry 18

Egret 20

The Penguins at Coney Island Aquarium 22

Itinerants 24

Shallows 25

Blizzard of '78 at Tucker Flats 26

stones in a stream 27

The Swallows

> *My heart in hiding*
> *Stirred for a bird, the achieve of, the mastery of the thing!*
> —Gerard Manley Hopkins

Custodians of an aerodynamic world,
  their zig-zag flights re-structure the air
    as they zoom by trailing teal tails.

They buzz the beach and tideline for eel grass,
  bleached cord grass, and other materials
    a nest to build in a raftered corner.

They settle not for nests under needles
  or leaves, delusions of shelter.
    Raftered barns or outbuildings their goal.

See how the swallows   swerve   swerve
  and veer off   off course   zag & zig
    at the last   loft   last instant

just before colliding into something!
  These are the wings with a mission.
    These are the zealots of the air.

They seem to be   darting   toward
  bedraggled flocks of wayward birds
    in desperate need of renewed power

for their ascents and wheeling agility.
  Is it these birds they are reaching for?
    They keep coming at the earth—

hierophants in split-tail gowns,
  chasubles on their shoulders,
    roof-corner celebrants.

It is to another parish
  their urgent under-songs pipe:
    Where are the listeners?

In the Realm of Flowers
> *And 't is my faith that every flower/Enjoys the air it breathes.*
> —Wm. Wordsworth

You can have your onion-collared
wrinkled-wilted yellow daffodils

and your weepy irises soiled umber
on their frayed fabric edges

nor would I settle for the lacework
of knuckled-root carrot-flowers

Paradigm of beauty, symbol of love—
its thorn a talon to rip out your heart

Give me the gentle geranium—
its pose so disarming on window sills

the humble honeysuckle—
its fragrance so evanescent and coy

coreopsis on gossamer stems
sweet-pea draped across dew-dipt fields

those clematis stars, envy of heaven
and red thread clover the whole world over

Dandelions—yellow and silver songs—
spin moons in orbit to seed suns

Dahlias lean toward sunlight to watch
cardinals loop the air like tossed bouquets

Look! Crocuses litter the lawn—
the gods left behind their cups of wine

Trumpet vines riff for hummingbirds—
those winged flowers doing the nectar dance

And isn't the poinsettia
the afterlife of a starfish

On the coldest day of the year
an empty coffee can is a flower

It's getting dark now and I'll need
the light of daffodils to lead me home

and I'll stash a fluffy ice-blue iris
in the top pocket of my sport jacket

I'll comprehend the cosmic chemistry
of Queen Anne's Lace and the starry night

I'll wake up in a field of buttercups
their radiance will see me through the day

If you find flowers frivolous
and ever more wither than bloom

then take a deep breath to savor
fragrance abiding in lilacs

If you prefer beach plum blossoms
try a handful of sand

They will need plenty of sun
and for a vase—the tide

Neap Tide

> *O sea...*
> *Would you the undulation of one wave, its trick to me transfer,*
> *Or breathe one breath of yours upon my verse,*
> *And leave its odor there.* —Walt Whitman

When these seaweed-slick stones slip and give
I will dance to the music of the spheres
for somewhere in these tidal sands
runs sifting secrets of the moon and sun.
Under the dune, when you listen,
you can hear clacking sounds of Corchaug bones
washing over quahog shells in the ebb-tide
and peace pipes lighting auroras of hope
while all the sands in the world, grain by grain,
nudge Atlantis toward the causeway of stars.

Given this world let my loose and scattered sands
collect like driftwood and seawrack heaved to shore.
Let my flawed initiatives lift from bins,
made straight as the seams on scallop shells.
Let my impugned ideals shine brighter
than sea anemones trapping the sun.
Let the emery edges of my heart
be smooth as clam shell buffed by surf.
But take away from me those oyster shells—
calcified twistings of outworn desires.

Like a sandpiper startled seaward
folding under its sticks of legs
cooling its wings over the waves
a flickering speck rising and diving
dipping away beyond the swells
listening to the sea's bruised tongue
echoing muffled syllables of terns
herons stripers snappers sea stars comets
I dash toward the cadence of the waves
where seahorses break from the gate of tides

Beachcomber

A sun-blazed ocean wave
builds up a wall of curve,
rolls its peeledgrapegreen ribs,
tosses splashwhite geysers,
collapses to bubbles of snow
scurryfooting over sands
sending their laundry out
to a voracious sea.
Attenuated polar bears
climb the steep bank
leaving shallows
of ordinary water.

Seagulls patrol their shore
while an ocean roars a roar
no jetport shall ever equal.
From the stasis of parade rest
caravans of noons
mount camelback dunes
in cones of continuum.
In slow slow motion truncated
my torched feet snag in sands—
zillions of granules of time—
to the gate of tides where an undertow
powers the sea's return voyage.

Clam Digger

No mountains here
No aspen forests
No desert flowers

This is where an ocean
runs out of salt
upon mere sands

This is where clams squiggle and slip
over down & under sea-polished sands
to hear the calm chords of tides

While tides keep their appointments
all the nereids and neptunes at sea
down their drinks in the cups of clams

The still life of a clamshell unhinges
to a dew-rise of liquor on its lip
and a heartbeat in its cup

All the clams in the sea
are the beats of time
waiting for the last day of summer

We know less about it
than the gunpowder seas on the moon
and the night moon sailing in the harbor

But this clam digger
anyhow
is not after the inside secret

or the beautiful beyond
of the last day of summer
This clam digger is a low-tide wader

to a sun-lit sandbar in the shallows
there to stand in wonder
to watch the tide come in

Casting for Sunlight in Flounder Town

Chalk-white boats bob like buoys on the bay
and beyond—a ghostly drift of fishing vessels.
Where are the boats that plied the sea for fish?
Where's THEO. ROOSEVELT's imposing prow?
The THEO. floats, sullen as a flounder,
its swollen lower lip a brim to the water.
Where's the PORTUGAL and its sea-warped mast?
The PORTUGAL still hauls in ocean fish;
the blood of the sea retches in its scuttle.
And seagulls, heartbeats in the swerve,
still swing swoop wheel pivot and dive,
fly down the runway of the sun
chasing a run of minnow and fry,
hover inches above pilings,
priests performing rituals,
light on tin roofs, huddle like ghosts,
and come into their own presence.

On Main Street merchants cast their lines
in vague hopes customers will take the bait.
Dally by GRAND-STAND's FIVE & TEN—
a checkerboard of counter-bins:
note pads, thumbtacks, LePage's Glue,
colanders, combs, and jars of gel wave set
in gooey green, pink, and lavender;
from a back room radio the Dorseys swing,
Benny Goodman wheedles marmalade blues,
Count Basie jumps at the Woodside.
Dally by LOUIE's CANDY KITCHEN—
a dark place lit by marble countertops
and ice cream milk-smell washed from dishes
drifts in the pressed tin ceiling air.
A & P produce clerks punch 5 cents stickers
on bunches of overripe bananas
and grocery clerks stock shelves with Lux,
Lava Soap, fly-paper, sardines, and Spam.

Hello to Henry Ritz and his DELI—
dill pickles and tang of salami
coffee aroma and linger of vinegar.
Hello to BUTLER'S butcher—his ham of a face
grins behind pallid pink hams hung from hooks.
There's TOWN HALL DINER waist deep in weeds;
waitresses weave and bob like ballet rehearsals.
There's KERR's Bakery, its applesauce cake
a flavor drawn from the stillness
sifting into town after 4:15 P.M.

Where have all the village lights gone?
Mrs. Magnuson, the fisherman's wife,
who kept a house tight as a sardine tin,
Mrs. Nucleo who beat a path downtown
to find her life in the Movies,
the bent-over woman in burlap skirts
who picked dandelions on our lawn,
Sam—four feet ten inches and fog horn voice
front and center every village parade,
Dennis Dice who alerted youth
to the truth of *Tempus Fu(d)git*
then died on a dime at sixty-five,
and Doc Ozone the merry mortician?
Down what streets do their steps fall now?

Flounder Town laid out like a fluke bone—
town under cover of the bay's salt breath.
Negative of weather your light filtered,
you lie like the Bottom remaining
after the Sea receded to the Deep.
Your sea-salted timbers teeth like barnacles.
Bay-Town, wind-whistled town, double exposure,
rise now, O rise now toward the sun!

Still Life with Whelk Shell and Coconut

Coiled spires and seams surrounding its shell
leave no clues of its seafaring secrets.
We look at a whelk shell in sheer wonder:

a nautical clock emptied of its works,
trumpet divested of its sea chanteys,
cell phone washed ashore from Triton's den,

or exquisite china from Neptune's table?
Listen! Listen to this mystery shell!
Before it curled up its toes
its life forgot to turn off the power

You're stranded on an uncharted island
where the coconut, a tusky nocturne,
brooded to form in the idle of time.

A six-haired goatee hangs from a pinched chin
of its woodsome gothic humanoid head.
An intense white light burns steady

in the grotto of its darkness.
Yet it has no lantern power.
Shake the shell. It clears its throat—
about to say something

Seagulls off Captree Basin

Where sandbars surprise fish
                seagulls wheel swing and hustle
pivot dive and sweep
                spin a dance of myth and wind.
Does the sea lure these gulls
                toward its undertow?
An undertow's deception
                cannot beguile these gulls.
These gulls rise unfold and hover
                seed root stem and petal
the sea's own gray flowers
                a toss and bouquet above the surf.
Some gulls fly landward
                to dunes their port-of-call.
These gulls strut their stuff
                like cool conventioneers
huddled in a hotel lobby
                their double-breasted suits
packed with cell phone numbers
                programs and Cuban cigars.
Tumblers of Aqua Johnny
                enticements up their sleeves.
Wheeler-dealers on the wing.
                But one forgets
or remembers himself
                flies off toward the sea
his eye cold as the ocean
                his cord legs stiffly tucked
in the bay of his tail.
                Poised on a shell of air
he twists his corn-grain beak
                ready to swoop
but angles toward the sun
                for other game.

Neck Road Idyll

1

The Long Island Sound a plate glass ocean
plied by a barge, compass needle loosened
from a center elusive as eel grass.
The Sound, a mouth, a language lost at sea
drifting to shore in fragile syllables.

Offshore rocks surface and submerge
in the slowest ballet of tides.
Most rocks go under at high tide.
As the tide goes out rocks rise to their places
a beach-proud jagged pier of boulder rocks:

Cradle Rock Lightning Rock Stubbed Toe Rock.
Further out—a mammoth rock—its spine visible
only at low tide, while at high tide
a sub-marine secret defying searches
from frustrated frog-stroking swimmers.

Found by some scan more subtle than sonar—
this rock rooted like the sea's own tusk.
When mounted, one wonders if it might rise,
lift its knees toward the high klieg lights,
trade routines with saltwater clowns.

Barnacle-hide and seaweed for hair,
this ridge-like hump a saddle for several.
Bell-buoys bell the ears of tadpole sailors,
those bareback riders who ride every light
and sound of summer—ride Elephant Rock.

2

We were the tadpole sailors
who took the old rowboat out
for a voyage to Guilford Shore
but inattentive to the tidal drift
we made it only to Applehurst Camp
where we ran out of saltwater,
the tidal creek receding to the sea,
our barnacled ship stranded on muck.
We waited over an anguished hour
for the return of the incoming tide
and a dejected row back to the dock
(and late for a birthday party.)

Yet Howie thought we were salts enough
to set out in his Chriscraft runabout
for a morning of fishing on the Sound.
In fog thick as Connecticut Chowder,
we anchored off the Point in a saddle of sea.
Bass, fluke, and weakfish not biting.
Monsters from the Deep flopped aboard:
two sea robins, a sand shark, and a ray.
Rubbery sand shark the color of fog,
primaeval head zippered with teeth.
Finally settled for a pail of porgies
for a grilled lunch that still taunts my palate.

3

With its arched roof a carapace,
its back porch staircase like pincers,
this cottage—warped floors, sunken porches—
leaned as against the bottom of a dock post,
a blue claw crab that would not take the bait,
cool customer mired in the salt marsh.

Gone—this cottage burned to the ground,
its timbers and creaks beyond conjuring.
Gone—the cracked croquet mallets and wickets,
and softballs like months-old grapefruit,
and badminton birdies crushed in the mad dash
for the dock and the best crab net.

Gone—the bright porches. Gone—the breakfast scene.
No more high tides under your breath:
'I don't want brown sugar on my corn flakes.'
Gone—the dim lamps that lit pinochle games
and the lights that flickered in thunderstorms.
Gone—the wind-rattled antique windows.

Where light refracted through warped window panes
angles and planes of light now pass unimpeded.
Low tide smells from marshes still linger here.
In a creek-side Tartarean stretch of dark muck
where you could lose a sneaker if not a foot,
fiddler crabs still hold concerts never heard.

4

Along Applehurst Creek where minnows
run from chimera of the Deep,
eel grasses, keeping time to the wind,
raise a marine anthem for us
who dance on sandbars.
When I paddle across the creek,
I find dragonflies sporting with mallow.
In the deep lungs of this salt marsh,
you can hear the fish breathing.
The marsh exhumes its vapors like rumors.
Terns, swallows, and clapper rails come and go,
but there's little firm footing here for me.
On the horizon's field of varied light
a train winds
            around the wetlands
stitching the edge of the creek
where the blue claw runs
with the rising tide
and my song for the whistle
                    lingering
in the still air
long after the train has gone by

Bay Light

Barrier beach six miles from the main shore
a long long haze-haunted sandland mirage
(fisherman's line lost in the surf)
cannot constrict the Great South Bay
runway for mallards and buffleheads.

Windmill wings whistle downwind,
rest on the under-runs of the bay,
Long after   noon the sun shimmers
its pointillist dance on silver water
teased by a breeze, the bay at brim level.

Within this expansive eye-reach
only a garvey remains, gently rocking,
its clammer raking the sea bottom
for last week's wages, last year's debts.
The bay at dusk becomes the sky's lagoon.

A few watts of light displace dusk
in the garvey's box-closet cabin—
from shore an oversized postage stamp,
a gold nugget set in silhouette
on a bay slipping into the pouch of night.

Voyages

When night slinks away and dawn tips its cap,
clouds scramble a calligraphy
discernible to the tadpole sailor
with a herring bone in his pocket,
a tea bag in his hand,
and a buoy belling in his ear,
as he stands stranded on the pier
watching the ship   drift   away   away   away
toward the realm of The Unknown,
never knowing that sailors lean over railings
and wonder why they ever left safe harbor
to be so far out at sea
burdened with a cargo of time
more arcane than horizons never reached

The Cry

pierced
our cabin
all night—

a
long
sharp

moan

Loneliness
leaving
the world

for the salt marsh
beside us,
finding

the throat
to unwind
its sound

At dawn
the sun
draws the mist

from the marsh
and I see
the sound

behind
the eye
and moon

of
the
loon

Egret

This water-edge apparition
   in this cattail marsh habitat
      lends part of its presence
         to an arc of light
            quietude its mode and motive
               its milkglass body a statuary
               its tight head wired
                  its eye a still pool

More than the sum of its geometry
   a stand   a pose   a promulgation
      image of stillness   pause of all music
      a sailsheet-white visitation
         its interior a throbbing empire

It stands on one of its stalk legs
   the other raised
      poised between two worlds
         tail more air than feather
            ball bearing body wound
               crane neck cocked
                  agate eye arrowed
                     blade of its horn beak precise

It moves—almost a sleight-of-wing—
   its right leg extends and mounts
      a slight rise   a knob of stubble
         its left leg perpendicular to the shallows
            time   its   toy

It rises—the dawn feather by feather
    Its wings re-arrange atoms in the air
       It measures angles for gardens
          fastens the flaps of tents
             opens gates and doors
                letting in more light
                    tunes the chords of harps and flutes
                      weaves a soundless symphony

In what furnace this form forged?
    In what ingot this loft refined?
        What quartz quarry pludered?
          What linen closet sacked?
            What light left dim?

Up from its stump
    it ascends
        fanning its wings
           and out goes
              its fire

The Penguins at Coney Island Aquarium

These penguins do not stir
when tourists "oooh" and "aaah."
These penguins read the signs of the ice
eons of glaciers and worlds ago
when they were the first sports
tobogganing through the Void
without a garden or workshop
in which to craft their poems and sagas.

Their bounds the bounce of their bobble-bodies.
One step looks like a sure loss of balance,
the next a snappy pivot to The Twist.
Their wonky-waddle totter-slippage walk
elicits chortles from those grandstanders
who know little of their dauntless valor—
their stance against the blow and bite of wind
in a raw frigid zone colder than ice.

I envy their impeccably tailored outfits,
their ultra-sophisticated manner,
the ease and cachet of their suave style,
even as now one cool dude leans on a rock
puffing on a mentholated Kool cigarette,
scented smoke swirling *je ne sais quoi*.

Some penguins wear sunglasses haute couture.
Some dine on Dover Sole and Haut Sauternes.
Others huddle on corners to compare stocks
and find a crisis in the rising price of ice
in the coastal precincts of East Antarctica.
I wonder whether their economy will tank
when I watch dames teeter-totter tiptoe
to neighbors to ask if one could spare a teabag.

Ever the epitome of resilience,
most are content to caper in their pools
like babes in a bubbly bathtub,
preen in the sun of any season,
and like modern pundits
keep an eye on the rising sea.

Itinerants

In their hooded black capes and bouffant shirts,
their heather mix jackets and composure,
their meditative manner and reserve,
refined pride and legs in jodhpurs tight,
who are we to say they do not
in their doddering deliberations
sort syllables from stones and pebbles,
read grass leaves in light of the weather,
collocate clay for compendiums,
ponder the mystery of existence?

They gather in groups on the lawn
like patrons standing outside a concert hall
waiting for the performance to begin.
In their nonchalant diffidence,
the costume of their countenance,
they seem poised to indulge in idle chatter.
Unruffled, the epitome of grace,
as though these connoisseurs of atmosphere
did not beat their wings seconds ago
against a recalcitrant wall of air.

Their gullets overloaded with gossip,
their wings labor again like oars,
sustainable flight to achieve.
They dare to steer toward the sound barrier
even as wearied wings recede to the rear
like stars falling from Orion's belt.
Stranger than the sound of heavy wet wash
wheeled out on a grinding rusted pulley,
their utterly unearthly cries
dismantle an astonished sky.

Shallows

The light of the moon on a trail:
the bottom of a brook
where the trout is barely seen

Blizzard of '78 at Tucker Flats

A crushed elderberry sky
pours dark purple wine
into oaken casks of vessels

What's left of reeds and rose mallow
pipewort and pickerelweed
hibernates in a salt marsh habitat

where last season split-tail swallows
flashed blue darted angled dove
rose toward nests for the night

In a world now dark-deep in silhouettes:
wind-whipped oaks & osprey nests on posts
rusted riggings & tackle-torn booms

Blizzard! The bite of the wind-driven snow
whiplashes your face blinds your sight
and daggers from the dens of chimera

Nor'easter-nasty winds lathe hulls
in sickle-swift   snow drifts
bound for an erratic voyage

neither out to sea
nor to far reaches in space
These ships sail toward an Icarian fate:

compass rudder and bow tilting starboard
engine torque belt slipping below
boiler plate leaking and the first to go

Fragile crystal music a hush band sound
Ghosts dance until the lights go out
Mallards burn like candles

stones in a stream

a toss of teeth spit out by Goliath
    pickled onions taking a shower
        where fragments of fallen stars end up

small-gauge asteroids tumbled from space
    little necks bubble-bathing in shampoo
        oysters calcifying in anti-freeze

walnuts toy deer crouch and kneel in
    eyes of marble performing surgery
        the loons' wild cries quenching a thirst

currents murmur:
    stones are thoughts
        left by bears

In language evocative and rich in detail, imagery, and reflection, Russell Steinke, the poet of TIDELINES observes, explores, and praises the particulars in, and even the linkages among, inanimate, florescent, avian, marine, and human domains. To a large extent, TIDELINES is essentially a meditative ode to the American Coastline and to the mystical lure of the sea. The Long Island Coastline was/is often a resource, force, and haunt for Russell's poetic perspectives.

In addition to tuning in to the music of various poets and to the hum of his own muse, Russell honed his craft within the following context. The help meet the cost of a college education, he worked a variety of jobs: for example, as shoe store custodian and U.S. Department of Interior cartographer and at an outdoor furniture factory and a brewery battling plant. After a brief stint in advertising, he decided on the field of education. While a SUNY educator, he taught undergraduate courses in English Literature I and II, Shakespeare, American Literature I and II, Hawthorne, and Modern Literature, and he presented several professional conference papers on Vaughan, Milton, Conrad, Stevens, and Mailer. Prior to the publication of TIDELINES, he published over sixty poems in various literary journals. During his tenure as an editor of LONG POND REVIEW, a literary journal, it was the recipient of several citations as Best Small Press by THE PUSHCART PRIZE. His idea of time well spent is reading and re-reading Stevens' poetry, Faulkner's fiction, Joyce's FINNEGAN'S WAKE, and comparable works of literary elan.

www.ingramcontent.com/pod-product-compliance
Lightning Source LLC
LaVergne TN
LVHW041513070426
835507LV00012B/1546